THE VOICE FROM THE CROSS

THE VOICE
FROM THE CROSS

Sermons on the Seven Words From the Cross

ANDREW W. BLACKWOOD, JR.

BAKER BOOK HOUSE
Grand Rapids, Michigan

PHOTOLITHOPRINTED BY CUSHING - MALLOY, INC.
ANN ARBOR, MICHIGAN, UNITED STATES OF AMERICA
1978

INTRODUCTION

The Seven Last Words fall into two groups. The first three Words relate to our Lord and others; the last four, to Christ and His Father. In dealing with each Word our son has thrown the stress on the divine, more than the human. As a pastor, formerly a chaplain, he knows the needs of men today, and how to meet them in Christ, supremely at the Cross.

This book differs from anything else in print. It ought to interest and help many pastors, seminary students, and lay readers. Each chapter brings a message from Golgotha, and shows the bearing on life today. These truths all are helpful at any time of year, and especially during the Christian harvest season before Easter.

If anyone wishes to find pardon, cleansing, and peace, with light and power for daily service, and hope for all the years to come, let him listen to the Seven Last Words. If he wishes to be transformed, and to be used in transforming others, let him give heed to the Voice from the Cross.

ANDREW W. BLACKWOOD, SR.

To
The Teacher

CONTENTS

1

THE PRAYER OF FORGIVENESS

Father, forgive them;
for they know not what they do.

LUKE 23:34

During the decisive hours of human history our dying Savior spoke seven times from the cross. The first word He uttered is a prayer of forgiveness: "Father, forgive them; for they know not what they do."

The only begotten Son of God died on the cross. Of all humanity our Savior alone has the right in Himself to address God as "Father." But Jesus went to His death that others might share this privilege. The Son of God endured a shameful cross so that we can become children of God. He became what we are; that we might become what He is. God is our Creator, our King, and our Judge. But He is more than all this. He is our Father, who aggressively seeks to adopt the one who is not yet His child. God's fatherhood is no mere passive feeling of benevolence toward the pleasant people in the world. On the cross our Lord shows that infinite love will go to infinite lengths to redeem us. The people of the world ought to stand in a relation of family affection with their almighty Creator. Since, obviously, this relationship does not exist widely in the world, God the Son entered into human life, and went to the cross, that we might be able to pray "Father."

The aim of all our striving within the Christian church is to become Christlike persons — children of the Heavenly

Father. As we listen to Christ during the central hours of
His work on earth, the first word we hear from His cross is
a prayer that the divine Father will forgive. Before a person
can speak such a word, forgiveness must be in his own heart.
The voice from the cross, crying down through the ages, calls
to us that it is a Christian's duty to forgive. Almost everyone
stands ready to forget, rather than forgive, the unintentional
slights and jostlings we undergo daily. But when a person
sets out with deliberate malice to do us harm, we are not
so eager to forgive. Yet, if we would be children of the
Heavenly Father, we must.

Jesus says, "Father, forgive them; for they know not what
they do." The crucifiers knew well that they were destroying
an innocent Man, but each of them had a plausible reason
for his act. A soldier, after all, must obey orders. The
governor must keep the peace. The high priest must protect
the people from blasphemy. So weak men worked together
to destroy the Son of God. They killed Him, but they could
not destroy Him. Even in death His love rose above their
hatred.

"They know not what they do." The New Testament word
for "sin" means literally "missing the mark." Though the
crucifiers had plausible reason for their act, they aimed in the
wrong direction; they missed the mark. When we sin we sel-
dom think of the final result of our action. Were it not for
the grace of God, the end result of human evil would be
spiritual death. Because God is love, He entered into the
whirlpool of human existence, to live with sinful men, and
to die for sinful men, with a prayer of forgiveness on His lips.

In happier days Jesus gave us the Lord's Prayer. By common consent this is the finest prayer ever uttered. Since our
Lord's day, thousands of devout thinkers have written books
and pamphlets about His words, but Jesus Himself made
only one recorded comment, "If ye forgive men their trespasses, your heavenly Father will also forgive you: but if ye

forgive not men their trespasses, neither will your Father forgive your trespasses" (Matthew 6:14-15). Needless to say, it is much easier to talk about forgiveness than it is to forgive. In His days as a Teacher our Lord taught us the duty of forgiveness. In dying as our Savior, our Lord forgave.

The cross of Christ is the heart of God's plan for saving the people of the world. It is not merely one more instance of man's brutality to man. God has taken this instrument of slow torture and death, and has made it into a vehicle of life and hope. We have a faith that centers in the Christ of the cross, a faith that calls us to become Christlike persons. Since the first word Christ spoke from the cross is one of forgiveness, we must take His word as a timeless command that we practice forgiveness when we suffer wrong.

For Whom Does Jesus Pray?

"Father forgive them." For whom does Jesus pray? Surely His prayer includes the soldiers who drove the nails into His hands and feet, who knelt at the foot of the cross, not in reverent sorrow, but to cast dice. Perhaps these were the same men who last night threw a purple robe about Him, and smote Him on the head with a reed, and spat upon Him, and offered Him mock worship. If any one so abused you, could you pray for his forgiveness? Jesus did.

We can understand why the soldiers were so savage. They were paid to be cruel. The cross was an instrument of political terror, and they were the men who must do the filthy work of crucifixion. They had to develop a thick callous over their hearts, or go out of their minds. We can understand the soldiers' action. Our Lord did more. He forgave.

Certainly He prays for the members of the mob who, the night before, had shouted, "Crucify him" (Mark 15:13). Now, as they pass Him by they sneer, "Thou that destroyest the temple, and buildest it in three days, save thyself, and come down from the cross" (Mark 15:29-30). These people in the mob had many troubles. When the High Priest him-self suggested that Jesus was the cause of their woes, they joined in a shout to get rid of this Rabble Rouser. Oh, they were stupid and easily led. But surely we should be able to understand. The Savior did more. He forgave.

Our Lord prays for the disciples who fled during the last night, when peril drew near. Certainly He prays for His friend Peter who denied his Lord. Again we can understand. We all have known the shock of physical danger. We all have been tempted to run away. Most of us have at times succumbed to the temptation. We can understand. The Redeemer did more. He forgave.

Christ includes Caiaphas and Herod and Pilate in His prayer of forgiveness. Can we not understand why they acted as they did? They were responsible authorities, placed in positions of influence precisely so that they could resist the pressure of the mob. They had received every advantage of birth and education and social position. They had tremen-dous power, which they needed if they were to carry out their duties. They knew all about the theory and the practice of justice, and they had sworn to enforce the law.

The chief priests, we are told, acted out of envy. But they held to a faith that was supposed to help them overcome self-centered desires. Pilate acted from fear of mob violence. A riot would be a black mark against his record. To avoid the black mark in the Emperor's book, Pilate blotted his name out of the Book of Life. We can understand why these moral weaklings failed in the time of testing. The Son of God did more. He forgave.

Christ prays for those immediately responsible for His suf-fering and death. But His prayer reaches far beyond the boundaries of Jerusalem, far beyond the Friday afternoon on which He died. Included in this prayer is a multitude which no man can number, of all nations, and kindreds and peo-ples, and tongues. Across the wide oceans, and down through the long centuries His prayer reaches, to embrace you when you have missed the mark. And, forgiveness will certainly be yours if you repent of your sins.

The Meaning of Forgiveness

When a person has done something to weaken or destroy the bond of love between you two, and you receive him back into the love that he has tried to wreck, then you have forgiven him. Similarly, divine forgiveness means that our heavenly Father takes into His family one who has rebelled against the love of God.

Forgiveness comes on two levels, that of sins and that of wrongs. In its relation to God, we call an evil act a sin. In relation to the neighbor who suffers because of this act, we call it a wrong. The two levels of forgiveness intersect in the life of a Christian. As our Lord tells us, if we would accept the forgiveness of sins, we must practice the forgiveness of wrongs.

The crucifiers knew that they were committing a wrong. Pontius Pilate declared, "I find no fault in this man" (Luke 23:4). After Jesus died, the centurion said, "Truly this man was the Son of God" (Mark 15:39). To condemn and destroy an innocent person is the lowest depth of wrong. Beyond all wrong, the crucifixion was the blackest sin in human history: for God was in Christ. God Incarnate stood before a man, and the man delivered God, when he had scourged Him, to be crucified.

Sin or wrong — the evil act drives a wedge between two persons. Only the one who has been wronged, or sinned against, can remove it. Extracting this wedge is painful. The forgiveness of your sins cost almighty God the cross.

The Forgiveness of Sins

At the dawn of human history, Adam and Eve expelled themselves from the Garden. Ever since that time, as people have sinned, they have in effect walked away from the love of

God. On the cross Jesus asks the heavenly Father to take the crucifiers back into His love. They have disowned their Father in Heaven. Jesus prays that He will receive them as His children.

When we try to understand the cross of Christ, and the ways in which divine love enters human life through our Savior's suffering, we stand face to face with mystery. This is scarcely surprising. The crucifixion is the central act of the encounter between God and man, and the most elementary fact of Christian experience is the mystery of God. When we attempt to understand the divine Being, and the ways of His Providence, we are trying to reach far beyond our grasp.

A scientific explanation of the cross is simply impossible. A scientist can explain the orbit of Neptune or the complicated workings of heredity. But he has no tools to measure and no words to express the mystery of the interaction between God and man. To understand, or come as close to an understanding as is possible, we must use poetry and parable, as the psalmist and the Savior did long ago.

An interpretation of the cross has been offered us in the beautiful parable given to us by Anselm of Canterbury in the Eleventh Century. The parable says in effect: Suppose we think of God as a great Banker, to whom each of us owes a debt that is too large to pay. We are without hope of meeting our obligation. But the Banker's Son says, "Father, let me pay the debt in full." The cross of Christ is the final payment.

Obviously, this is not an explanation. It is a parable which has proved wonderfully helpful for the past eight centuries. Most Christians today believe that the meaning of the cross lies in the direction where the parable points. But a complete explanation of the power and the glory of our Redeemer's life and sacrificial death must ever escape us. Need we understand nutrition in order to eat? Must we understand the Atonement before we can be saved? Centuries

before Anselm of Canterbury people were living Christlike
lives. The forgiveness of sin was a vital fact in human experience long before theologians began trying to explain it.

By way of the cross God offers His forgiving love. What is
man's response. Once a troubled jail warden asked that question of two brave men. Terrified by a midnight earthquake,
he ran to them and asked, "Sirs, what must I do to be
saved?" (Acts 16:30). They might have given him a host of
moral injunctions, or a list of religious ceremonies. They
might even have told him to go out and integrate his per-
sonality. But under the guidance of the Holy Spirit, they
said, "Believe on the Lord Jesus Christ and thou shalt be
saved" (Acts 16:31). Faith is man's response to God's forgiving love.

What is faith? Surely it means holding the right opinions
about God, but it includes more than a set of ideas held in
isolation from daily conduct. Faith is belief strong enough
for action. It looks in two directions. Looking backward,
faith sees all the evil that separates man from God. Faith
gathers together the sorry mess of guilt and carries it to our
Father, asking Him to lay it on the cross where the Savior
died. When sins are forgiven, faith looks forward to a new
life, a redeemed life, a Christlike life.

On the cross our Savior threw open the door of God's forgiveness. Faith is man's step across the threshold. We do
not save ourselves; we must be saved. If anyone doubts our
need for the Savior, let me commend to him a thoughtful
reading of the daily paper. The world is cursed with sin
today, the same kind of sin that nailed Jesus to the Cross.
Our Lord endured the cross long ago to offer us God's forgiveness. "God commendeth his love toward us, in that, while
we were yet sinners, Christ died for us" (Romans 5:8).

Most of those for whom Jesus prayed did not want his love
and forgiveness, just then. A scant few hours after, as the
disciples were huddled together in their misery, Christ came

to them and told them that, though they had failed Him in His hour of need, He would never fail them. They had, as it were, closed the door of divine love. He opened it again, and they gladly entered in. Six weeks later, Peter and the other disciples stood boldly on the street corner in Jerusalem to proclaim their faith in Jesus, crucified yet alive and at work in the world. That day three thousand converts entered the Church. Is it too much to hope that some of the mob which so recently had howled for Jesus' blood were numbered among the three thousand? Dare we hope that in time even Herod and Caiaphas and Pilate came to realize that the door of God's love stands open for the one who by God's grace is willing to enter in?

The Forgiveness of Wrongs

The door is still open. But after one has entered, what then?

The Savior is a good Captain who leads the troops into the position that we are to occupy. He teaches forgiveness, and He died that we might be forgiven. It follows then that our duty as Christians is to forgive.

We often see forgiveness within the home. When a little child does something that would be terribly wrong for an adult, we are not overly aroused. We try to help the child to understand what is right and what is wrong, but the bond of love is not even stretched.

After a while, though, the child is old enough to know the difference between right and wrong — say twelve or fourteen. Then, if the child does something morally evil, the parents know something of the sadness that must often fill the heart of God. Let us say that the child tells his parents a deliberate lie. They want to trust him, but they cannot. He has weakened the bond of confidence that ought to unite the members of a family. Christian parents cannot laugh away any wrong. They do everything in their power to help the child understand why there must be truthfulness within the home. Where it is possible, they expect the child to correct the result of his falsehood. If punishment is called for, they administer punishment. But when the child comes to himself, he realizes that he still is surrounded with the love of his parents. He has mocked their love, but it is greater than his wrong. He has wronged them. They have forgiven.

In a time of doubt and uncertainty, like today, it is all-important that we Christians keep open the doors of love. About us, doors of understanding, sympathy, and tolerance are being slammed and bolted. If we manifest the spirit of Christ, we try to understand where others refuse to think. We try to sympathize where others condemn. We try to love where others hate. Like our Lord, we forgive.

Remember, the Savior offered His forgiveness to others before they wanted it. You cannot force another person to accept your friendship. But you can stand ready and willing to receive an enemy as a friend as soon as he is willing. That is forgiveness.

Quite naturally and quite rightly we are friendly with those whom we like, those who are friendly to us. On the cross Jesus teaches us also to extend our friendship to those whom we are tempted to hate, those whom we might otherwise fear and mistrust. The Redeemer's first word from the cross is a prayer not for those who are lovable, but for those who are thoroughly detestable.

Forgiveness does not mean our modern habit of flabby-mindedness in which we flatten out all distinction between right and wrong. The closer we draw to Christ, the greater grows our hatred for evil. Along with our hatred, love for the sinner ought to grow in our hearts. The sinner is the victim of evil. As Christians, we help him to become the victor over evil.

Forgiveness means opening the doors of love. It does not mean abandoning one's intelligence. If a child plays with matches and burns down the garage, you forgive him. But you do not proceed to give him a blowtorch. To be sure, he wants a blowtorch, and he cries for it piteously, but in your love you say no. You have forgiven. You love the child. But you try to love him intelligently.

So, in this world where we Christians are commanded to forgive, we sometimes must use physical force. We all agree that bank robbery is a grave wrong. When someone robs a bank, we cannot arrest and punish bank robbery. We must, if we can, arrest the person who committed the act. Having arrested him, we cannot turn him loose to repeat his wrong. We must help him, and others who are tempted, to realize that some kinds of conduct are not tolerable. If we can discover something better than prisons to teach this lesson, we should turn to the better method. In the meantime we must use the tools we have.

Forgiveness of wrong demands something far harder than opening the prison doors. It demands that we carry on all the constraints of society in a spirit of Christlike love. Our faith demands that we show intelligent concern in what happens behind the walls of the penitentiary. It requires us to do our utmost to see that imprisonment is a chance for the convict to find himself, not merely an opportunity for society to wreak vengeance upon him. And when he is released, forgiveness means that we shall help a brother accept the responsibilities of freedom. Where we have the spirit of forgiveness, we still must have law. If, for some, law means physical restraints, for us Christians law means the moral restraints of love. Whether we like the idea or not, our Lord's first word from the cross bids us offer our love to the unlovable.

Each of us prays that one day, pray God it may come soon, we shall have a reign of law among nations, as today we have it within the nation. One step that each of us can take toward the coming of that day is to cleanse his own heart from hatred for those persons whose actions he must hate. They know not what they do. Each of us can pray that God will show others where they are wrong, that He will move them to repent, and that He will forgive their sin. Meantime, our Savior tells us that we too must stand ready to forgive.

2

THE PROMISE OF LIFE

Verily I say unto thee,
Today shalt thou be with me in paradise.

LUKE 23:43

Three men died on Calvary. One was the divine Savior of the world; the other two were spiritual failures, thieves. One thief made a last, grisly jest: "If thou be Christ, save thyself and us." The other rebuked him, and turning to Jesus said, "Lord, remember me when thou comest into thy kingdom." The Savior answered, "Verily I say unto thee, Today shalt thou be with me in paradise."

"Today." The conversation took place on a Friday afternoon. By nightfall, all three of the speakers were dead. As they spoke, each knew that the moment of his physical death was at hand. Christ's promise to the penitent thief meant that by Friday night they two would be together in the presence of the heavenly Father.

Some believe that following the moment of death the soul sleeps until the time of the great resurrection. Others believe that before one can enter paradise there must be a period of cleansing in purgatory. When I discuss our Lord's promise to the dying thief with those who hold either of these beliefs, they tell me that the thief was a special instance of divine grace, that the promise was made to one sinner, and not to every sinner who faces death with faith in Jesus Christ. If that were the case, why should the conversation be recorded in the New Testament?

In thinking about the life to come, we cannot test our hypotheses, then come back and report. Our faith must reach beyond the limits of our sight. Through the Scripture, God has revealed to us as much as we need to know about eternal life. The bulk of the Scriptural evidence is summed up in the Westminster Shorter Catechism: "The souls of believers are at their death made perfect in holiness, and do immediately pass into glory; and their bodies, being still united in Christ, do rest in their graves, till the resurrection." In other words, Jesus spoke to one Christian from the cross, but through that one He speaks to every Christian.

"Today shalt thou . . ." The promise came to a dying man. Within a few hours the thief was dead. Perhaps his body was buried in the potter's field. Perhaps, like Jesus, he had a friend who took the body to a nearby tomb. Each of us in turn must go through this process of death, when the heartbeat is stilled and we breathe no more. Following death we Christians believe that the soul, the essential "thou," enters into life.

Concerning the destiny of the soul there are only three possibilities conceivable to the human mind. First is our Christian belief. Following physical death the soul continues its individual existence. Then there is the opinion that it becomes something or someone else. Most of the Hindus, for example, believe that the individual is like a cup of water scooped up from the ocean. After many incarnations, when the cup finally breaks, the water pours back into the sea, or in other words, the soul is absorbed into the All-Soul. The third view is that when the body dies the soul dies along with it. Survival, change, extinction: nothing else is possible. Our Savior teaches the first. When your earthly life is over, you will continue to be yourself down through eternity.

"With Me in paradise." You will continue to be yourself, but stripped of all that is base and ignoble, while all that is strong and clean in you will be glorified and intensified.

In paradise you will be with Christ, who came into earthly life to redeem you, to save you, to transform you into a child of the living God. Jesus said, "Ye must be born again" (John 3:7). During earthly life we know spiritual birth, infancy, and adolescence. In the life of the world to come we shall know spiritual maturity. That world of spiritual perfection is paradise.

Only this once is it recorded that Jesus spoke of "paradise." The word was common enough in Jesus' day among the rabbis, who had many and sometimes strange interpretations of paradise. In using the term our Lord does not depart from the rest of His teaching about life after death. The majority of Protestant scholars understand this word from the cross to be simply another way of saying "heaven." Our Lord has much to tell about heaven in the course of His teaching. The heart of it all is, "If I go and prepare a place for you, I will come again and receive you unto myself; that where I am, there ye may be also" (John 14:3). We have the Savior's promise that when earthly life is over, a different quality of life is waiting. This is spiritual life, eternal life, life with our Redeemer. This is paradise.

The Promise to a Thief

If ever a man had reason for despair, it was the dying thief. He had lived a life of disobedience to God and rebellion against society. He confessed that his execution was just, the due penalty of his deeds. Before him lay the ebbing of vitality, and then the looming horror of the shades. To the human eye his condition was utterly hopeless. But through him our Lord has brought us a message of expectancy and radiant hope, when the outlook without faith would be only bleak and awful.

Sometimes we talk as if heaven were a reward for our good conduct on earth. Here on the cross, dying beside Jesus, is a person whose conduct has been anything but good. To him, a moral weakling, a spiritual failure, Jesus opens wide the gates of paradise.

We have little trouble in believing that good people live into eternity. On the cross our Savior tells us that the way is open also for bad people. If we believe that once, long ago, God welcomed a criminal into eternal life, then the rest of us, who are not so bad as we could be, and not so good as we should be, can look into the future with hope.

Receiving the Promise

Jesus gave His promise of life to the penitent thief, not because he deserved it, but because God is love, and by faith the dying man had laid hold on God's love. We do not buy immortality with our good works. What can we offer that is worth what we hope to receive? Let me illustrate. A small child comes to the Washington Monument with his life's savings clutched in his hand. He goes to the guard and offers to buy the Monument. Unclasping his fist, he shows thirty cents. The kindly guard must explain. First, some things are not for sale. Second, if the Monument were for sale, thirty cents would not be enough to buy it. Most important of all, the child does not need to buy the Washington Monument; he already owns it. Everyone whose spirit is exalted and whose patriotism is deepened when he sees the Monument owns everything that such a memorial can give.

The prophet Isaiah, speaking about our good works, said, "All our righteousnesses are as filthy rags" (Isaiah 64:6). Though some rags are more filthy than others, still none are fit to wear at a banquet with the King. Yet the King says, "Take My spotless coat of righteousness, and wear it into My palace." By our own righteousness we cannot buy our way into heaven. By faith we can accept the gift of Christ's righteousness, as did the dying thief.

How did the thief know that Christ is able to guide a believer through death and into life? It is strange indeed that anyone should say to a man who is being executed as a criminal, "Lord, remember me when thou comest into thy kingdom." How did the thief recognize his King when others saw only a laughingstock? Jesus wore no trappings of royalty. All but a few of His subjects had turned and fled. Of course there was a sign over His head, "This is the King of the Jews," but the sign was meant in derision; for people do not crucify their King. Or do we?

All that the eye of flesh could see was a dying Man. But, it is with the eye of faith that the thief sees Jesus and decides, "Here is a Man whom I can trust. I believe His claim. He is my King. My only hope is to surrender myself to Him." The thief did not fully comprehend God's plan of salvation. He could not understand the way in which the Savior had taken his sin — and yours — unto Himself. But he could surrender himself, with all his need and problems to Christ. And that is where faith begins in every believer. Faith is a wholehearted trust in Christ, a casting of all our cares on Him, and full surrender to Him.

The dying thief has only a few hours more to live. His whole body is an indescribable ache. His hands and feet are stabbing flames of pain. His throat begs for a few drops of water. Ahead of him lies only more anguish, and then what? After he has committed himself to the Lord, the pains in his body burn just as they did before, but now the thief has something he has always lacked. Now he faces the unbearable future with hope, hope that Jesus is the Christ, the Lord of life, who cares for the individual sinner and welcomes him from this life into the world to come. For the remaining few hours of earthly torture, the dying thief lives his faith that Jesus Christ is King.

The Promise Today

Two thieves, side by side, endure the same kind of pain. Through their burning, bleary eyes, they see Another, suffering what they must endure. The magnetism of Christ attracts them, but His is spiritual magnetism that one can accept or reject. Each thief must decide for himself whether he will turn to his Savior or turn away. One contemptuously spurns Jesus. The other sees in Him the Promised Savior-King, and asks if he may become a subject. The King welcomes the new convert into the tiny band of believers. Ever since that time, as Christians have faced the pains of death, we have been able to look beyond the tragedy and into paradise.

We hold a faith that teaches us how to die. I have been with several hundred people during the course of their last few hours or days on earth. With many of these friends I have discussed what lies beyond. I can report that those who face the future with Christ look forward with hope, while those who enter the uncertainties of death without Him show at best a brave resignation, at worst a sickening, heartbreaking fear. We have a faith that teaches us to die in confidence that our Lord keeps His promises. Even more important, our faith teaches us how to live.

Certain of our critics to the contrary, Christianity is not a matter of eating pie in the sky by and by. It means becoming by faith a child of the heavenly Father, a brother or sister of the Lord Jesus Christ. This act of faith takes place on earth. Sometimes, as with the dying thief, faith comes at the end of a person's mortal life. Ideally, a person becomes a Christian as soon as he is old enough to understand what it means to accept Christ as his Savior.

As children of God we do our best to act the part, here and now, looking always to Jesus, the Author and Finisher of our faith, always looking forward, always looking up. And when our days on this planet are done, we still look forward and up, into life. Our Christian hope does not grow in a vacuum; it grows and develops out of our basic commitment. If Jesus Christ is what we believe Him to be, if He does what He promises to do, what can we do except hope?

Each of us must decide for himself whether he will accept the promises of Christ, or look elsewhere for the answer to life's deepest questions. In coming to a decision, we have something to guide us that the penitent thief did not have. We have the accumulated experience of the saints in all the ages who possessed the faith that Jesus Christ is the Savior, the trustworthy Guide through life. These people have died, physically, unwavering in their faith that their Lord would lead them into life.

Is Jesus Christ the kind of Person whom you can trust? Should you put your faith and hope in Him? Will you commit yourself to Him? These are the central questions of life. No one else can answer them for you.

Two thieves were confronted with a choice. The same choice faces you today. The thief who made the right choice and the saints through the ages, found that the decision for Christ brings forgiveness for the past, peace for the present, and hope for the future.

3

THE WORD OF KINDNESS

He saith unto his mother, Woman, behold thy son!
Then saith he to the disciple, Behold thy mother!

JOHN 19:26-27

At the foot of the cross stood Mary, the mother of our Lord, with Mary the wife of Cleopas, Mary Magdalene, and the disciple John. Our Lord, who read so well the human heart, knew the anguish that was rending His mother. What could He say to ease her pain? How could He explain to her that the cross is central to God's plan of salvation? Wisely He did not try, at the time. Rather, in typical kindness, He took care of His mother's present, immediate need. "He saith unto his mother, Woman, behold thy son!"

Then Jesus turned to His beloved disciple John, and asked him to make practical provision for Mary, as long as might be necessary. He asked him to express his love for Christ in terms of living-space within the home, and making all the petty adjustments that are necessary when an outsider becomes a member of the family.

The first word from the cross concerns our Lord's enemies. The second welcomes a stranger into friendship. The third shows our Savior's love for one who has always loved Him. Some Christians find it easy to be thoughtful of their brothers in the central Congo, and to pray fervently for the salvation of souls that are ten thousand miles away. This is, of course, an essential part of our faith. But it will never take the place of love for those who are close at hand.

Home is the best place on earth to practice Christian love. We have no quarrel with the old saying, "Charity begins at home." But every time someone says it to me, he really means, "Charity ends at home." The Christian must vigorously dissent from such a conclusion.

On the cross our Savior died for the sins of the world. Yet as we listen to His voice from the cross, calling down through the ages, we hear Him pray for those who crucified Him, accept a thief into the kingdom of faith, and express His practical concern for a lonely, frightened woman who loved Him. In other words, Christ cares not so much for the masses of humanity as for the persons who, one by one, compose the mass.

Thanks be to God that the Church today is thinking in world-wide terms of her responsibility. Thanks be that we are concerned about the global scope of Christianity. Global love is vast and important, but dangerously impersonal. It can never take the place of kindness to the individual. In His third word from the cross, our Lord underscores what He taught during the years of His ministry. It is our task as Christians to care for people one at a time, to think about their needs, and to translate our thoughts into action.

Jesus' Debt to Mary

In the mystery of His Incarnation, the eternal Christ became a helpless Child, who depended upon His mother for physical and spiritual sustenance. When God became Man, He took no half-way measures. He went through the helplessness of every child, the development in body, mind, and soul that each of us has known. As Jesus was growing, someone taught Him to behold the lilies of the field and the birds of the air. Someone taught Him to observe so keenly the pathos and drama of village life, the silly pomposities of little people, and the incredible heroism with which unknown folk bear the unbearable. The Son of Man saw life with all the sensitivity of a woman, and that woman was Mary.

Once Mary heard a promise concerning her Son: "He shall be great, and shall be called the Son of the Highest: and the Lord God shall give unto him the throne of his father David: and he shall reign over the house of Jacob for ever; and of his kingdom there shall be no end" (Luke 1:32-33). Now she sees this promise fulfilled in a cross.

We need not think about the angels, the shepherds, and the wise men to measure the depth of Mary's grief. How would you feel if it were your son suffering so hideously? That is how Mary felt, or at least as close as we can come to imagining the depth of her grief.

> For His people's sins chastised
> She beheld her Son despised,
>   Bound and bleeding 'neath the rod;
> Saw the Lord's Anointed taken,
> Dying desolate, forsaken,
>   Heard Him yield His soul to God.
>
> Near Thy cross, O Christ, abiding,
> Grief and love my heart dividing,
>   I with her would take my place:
> By thy guardian cross uphold me,
> In thy dying, Christ, enfold me
>   With the deathless arms of grace.

As we look at the scene of utter tragedy, which is relieved only by our Savior's compassion, an insistent question rises: Why was it necessary that John provide for Mary? In the normal course of events, Mary would make her home with one of her other children: James, Joses, Judas, Simon, or one of the daughters. But our Lord knew, and Mary knew, that for the immediate future at least, she would be more at home with John than with one of her own family.

We must picture a household divided. The Gospels tell us,

briefly but pointedly, that Jesus' brothers did not believe in Him. Like almost everyone else in Nazareth, they were too familiar with Him to believe that He was anything more than a wandering Rabbi. When Jesus said, "A man's foes shall be they of his own household" (Matthew 10:36), He was talking from sad experience. We gather from the Gospel record that Jesus' brothers thought Him out of His mind. Mary's loyalty to her eldest Son divided her from the rest of the family. During the next few months a sympathetic disciple would be closer to Mary than her own sons and daughters.

Our friends of the Roman Catholic Church have a different understanding of the reason why Mary was homeless until Jesus provided her a home with the beloved disciple. They believe that the brothers and sisters of our Lord were really step-brothers and step-sisters, possibly cousins. Surely Matthew, Mark, Luke, and John were quite capable of saying "step-brother" had they desired, yet when they refer to our Lord's brothers they call them "brethren." The alteration of the clear teaching of Scripture has come about because of a belief in the perpetual virginity of Mary. Coupled with the belief has come a gradual elevation of Mary's place in Catholic practice until today she stands only a step below her Son.

To an outsider it appears that the Roman Catholic worships the Virgin Mary. This the Roman Catholic denies. He explains that he worships God alone, but he offers to Mary veneration, beyond that offered to any other saint. He asks Mary and the other saints to intercede with Christ for him. Indeed, he finds it difficult to understand why we Protestants do not the same.

At the time of the Reformation, we Protestants went back to the Scripture as the final authority in matters of faith and practice. God has revealed Himself in the Bible. He has not answered all of our questions there, but He has told us what we need to know and do in order to be Christians. The Bible account of Christianity says nothing about veneration for the mother of our Lord, nothing about prayers that the saints intercede for us. Rather we read, "There is one God, and one mediator between God and men, the man Christ Jesus" (I Timothy 2:5). We believe that God became Man, in Jesus Christ, to mediate betwixt divinity and humanity, and we accept the statement of Scripture that no further mediator or mediatrix is necessary.

Sometimes, unhappily, we are so busy being Protestant that we forget to be Christian in our attitude toward those with whom we must disagree. We show no love for Christ by hating Roman Catholics or anyone else. If we see that others are mistaken in their religious practice, throwing stones will not correct the matter. Only love can heal the wounds within the earthly Body of Christ.

In His third word from the cross, our Lord tells us what Christian love means. It is neither a vaporous sentiment, nor a matter of romantic emotion. It is the practical expression of thoughtful kindness in meeting immediate human needs. Jesus owed a debt of gratitude to Mary, His mother. In the cruel suffering of the cross He remembered to express His gratitude. In the agony of death, He remembered to be kind.

Expressing Our Gratitude Today

We wish to express our gratitude to God for Mary and for the Son whom she brought into the world. We are among the generations of those who call her blessed. We thank God for the courage that enabled her to accept the heaviest responsibility any woman ever bore. We thank God for the bravery that led her to the cross when all but one of the men had fled. How can we express our gratitude? Jesus has some plain words on the subject of devotion to Mary. "It was told him by certain which said, Thy mother and thy brethren stand without, desiring to see thee. And he answered and said unto them, My mother and my brethren are these which hear the word of God, and do it" (Luke 8:20-21). Where is the mother of Christ today? Where are His brothers? In heaven, to be sure. If we wish to do the will of Christ, we shall also look for His mother and His brothers living across the tracks or in the house next door. When we are moved by Christian love to be considerate of the one who is in need, doubt, uncertainty, fear, or any other distress, we are serving Christ, expressing our gratitude to God for all the human agents who brought us our faith.

In the course of time, Jesus' brother James became a Christian, and then Bishop of the Church in Jerusalem. James writes the most compelling message of practical Christianity in the entire New Testament. "If a brother or sister be naked, and destitute of daily food, and one of you say unto them, Depart in peace, be ye warmed and filled; notwithstanding ye give them not those things which are needful to the body; what doth it profit? Even so faith, if it hath not works, is dead, being alone" (James 2:15-17). Mary's sons had learned well their lesson. Our faith reaches beyond the stars, but we must practice it on the surface of the earth.

Christian faith, the kind Jesus lived till the end of His days, is concerned about the practical problems our friends and enemies face. A Christian cares about the sick, the imprisoned, the hungry, the homeless. As James warns us, faith cannot be expressed in words alone. Words are a wonderful invention, but they will not feed a hungry child. In speaking to Mary and John, Jesus reminds us to express our faith in terms of practical thoughtfulness, not only for the enemy and the stranger, but for those who are close at hand.

The guiding principle of Christian kindness is the Golden Rule: "All things whatsoever ye would that men should do to you, do ye even so to them" (Matthew 7:12). Some will say, "The Golden Rule is my religion," but Christians know better. Christianity is more than an ethical code; it is a personal relationship with almighty God, brought about through faith in the Lord Jesus Christ. God gave us our faith to help us become His children, both in thought and in deed. A Christian holds beliefs about Christ in order that he may become a Christlike person, and Christ our Lord is kind.

Kindness, thoughtfulness, consideration, courtesy, love — these are the final earthly results of Christian faith. Is the Church today producing these results? Sometimes we go about trumpeting the failures of Christianity so loudly you would think that Jesus Christ had lived and died in vain. There is no room for smugness. Our Leader is still well ahead of the followers. But we ought to thank God for the ten thousand times ten thousand saints on earth who are following Christ today, in thought and in act.

Instead of looking throughout the world for examples of Christian kindness, we can look at one congregation. This is a middle-sized congregation in a middle-sized city. The members often think they have more than their share of difficult problems, but most churches think so. In the pastor's file cabinet is a folder marked "Deacons." A typical letter from the folder reads:

Dear Pastor,

Please express my thanks to the member of the Board of Deacons who came to call last Thursday evening. I am sorry, but I do not remember his name. I can't remember much of anything since my illness began.

It seems that writing is just about the hardest work I do. But I had to write to tell you how grateful I am.

Sincerely,

. . . .

"It seems that writing is just about the hardest work I do." For this person, each letter on the page brings a pain of its own. But she knows such a depth of gratitude that she willingly endures the pain, to express her thanks to a complete stranger who cares enough about lonely old people to give an evening to visiting. If the lonely old woman were your mother, you would be choked up with gratitude toward the friendly deacon who came to call on her. Christ is as grateful for this act of thoughtfulness toward one of His friends as He would have been for a visit to His own mother.

Without calling attention to what they are doing, some of the good Christians within the church are carrying a message of friendship and faith to the children in the State School for the feeble-minded. These Christians cannot give large sums of money, but they give what is worth more than anything purchasable. They give time. They take time to be friendly with those who have few friends.

Strong men and women guide children and young people in the community. Willingly they give up their leisure hours to the work of Christian education, in its broadest sense. They take time to study and prepare the eternal message of salvation in a form that today's young people can understand.

The cases of practical Christian love within the home are too numerous to mention. Parents go without what they want and need in order that their children may receive an education. Young couples stay cramped in tiny apartments, rather than moving to more spacious quarters, so that they can meet their parents' hospital bills. Brother denies himself that he may care for brother. Only when Christians fail to act like Christians within the home do people pay much attention.

Within the organization of the Church are many conflicting viewpoints about every issue that arises. Yet, as Christians disagree, they continue to respect one another, and to work together. Among the congregation are people in many different professions and industries. Almost all of them say that their daily toil is an opportunity to practice their faith. They have no use for a Gospel that operates only one day a week.

They believe that Jesus Christ came to redeem us from sin and to transform our lives wherever we may be, in the factory, the schoolroom, the marketplace, or the home.

The congregation mentioned is no glowing exception to the rule. It is just about typical. Wherever you go, you can find Christians who are striving constantly to express their faith in action. Our faith comes from the heavenly Father, through Jesus Christ, and into our lives. As an electrical circuit must be complete before it can operate, so the spiritual circuit of Christianity must be grounded in the life of somebody else. The Savior's third word from the cross tells us that the Christian is thoughtful of the other person. The Christian does for the other person what he would wish if the positions were reversed.

Suppose you were a lonely, frightened woman, not welcome among your own children. What would you wish others to do? Jesus did it. Suppose you were a member of a religious minority. Suppose your skin were darkly pigmented. Suppose you were in a state hospital, or a prison, or a tuberculosis sanitorium, or some other institution. What would you ask of your fellow man? Above all else, you would wish to be treated as an individual, valued as an individual, loved as an individual. You would ask your fellow man to treat you as a person, not a case. You would want him to be kind.

4

THE CRY OF DERELICTION

> *Eloi! Eloi! lama sabachthani?*
> *which is, being interpreted,*
> *My God! my God! why hast thou forsaken me?*
>
> MARK 15:34

"My God! my God! why hast thou forsaken me?" Of all the seven words from the cross, this is the most puzzling. Had the Father actually forsaken His Son? Or had Jesus lost, for a time, the consciousness of His Father's presence?

If God watches over the falling sparrow, though the sparrow is not aware of the fact, surely He beheld and cared while His only begotten Son suffered and died. For at least a blinding moment, our Savior "descended into hell." He sought the Father and could not find Him. He endured the final tragedy of sin in human life, which is separation from God.

With bated breath our fathers spoke of the fourth word from the cross as "the cry of dereliction," the cry of One who feels utterly, utterly lost. The cry means that man's ultimate misery — separation from God — has penetrated to the very heart of the Holy Trinity. It means that God Incarnate has entered completely into man's condition; that Christ has experienced life at the bottom of the heap; that He knows pain, loneliness, discouragement, and despair. It means that our divine Savior, who sits at the right hand of God the Father almighty, knows what it means to feel forsaken by God.

The fourth word from the cross is a source of hope to us today. If sometimes we echo our Savior's despair, we know

41

that God hears us, though we cannot hear Him. We believe that history has already reached its ultimate depth. However hopeless our future may look, it can never again descend to the black emptiness of the Friday afternoon when God Incarnate cried, "Eloi! Eloi! lama sabachthani?"

The cry of dereliction is one of the few places in the New Testament where we have the exact syllables that passed Jesus' lips. He usually spoke in Aramaic. The Evangelists wrote in Greek. We read the Gospel in English. We can be sure that there is good reason why Mark recorded Jesus' words as "Eloi! Eloi! lama sabachthani?"

In the first place, the remark that follows would be meaningless without the exact quotation: "And some of them that stood by, when they heard it, said, Behold, he calleth Elias" (Mark 15:35). Anyone who has ministered to the dying knows the difficulty of understanding a person's last, gasping words. When Jesus said, "Eloi!" some thought that He was calling for Elijah to return and usher in the Messianic kingdom.

A second reason is a reminder that Jesus, even in the moments of utmost despair, yet clung to His faith. For this cry from the cross is a quotation from the ancient hymnbook of the Jewish people. These are the opening words of the 22d Psalm. When we wish to refer to a hymn, we quote the first line; we do not speak a number. Jesus did just the same.

He says in effect, "I do not understand all this. I have lost the path. But others before me have lost their way, and the heavenly Father has found them." He suggests that His friends and enemies at the foot of the cross think deeply on the message of the 22d Psalm. In words that are prophetic of the cross, the psalmist sings:

> I am poured out like water,
> And all my bones are out of joint:
> My heart is like wax;
> It is melted in the midst of my bowels.

My strength is dried up like a potsherd;
And my tongue cleaveth to my jaws;
And thou has brought me into the dust of death.
For dogs have compassed me:
The assembly of the wicked have enclosed me:
They pierced my hands and my feet.
I may tell all my bones:
They look and stare upon me.
They part my garments among them,
And cast lots upon my vesture.

This is the reality of the moment. This is a literal description of Jesus' condition. But, others before Christ, and others since, have been deserted by man, and without the *feeling* that God knows or cares. Just as the darkness makes it impossible to see the solid object before us, so sometimes discouragement makes it impossible for us to realize that God is at hand. To carry us through such moments, we Christians have knowledge beyond that of the psalmist. The cross has become reality. Beyond the cross lies the resurrection. Even with this knowledge, Christians often are discouraged and lonely, and feel God-forsaken.

The psalmist begins his song in the night on a note of utmost despair, but he carries his despair to God. While feeling that God had abandoned him, yet he prays, "My God! my God! why hast thou forsaken me?" If we would follow the psalmist in this regard and carry our present thoughts to God, instead of waiting until we have thoughts that are more proper, then our faith might help us, as it helped the psalmist and the Savior long ago, to overcome discouragement, setbacks, and despair.

Here is a prayer, uttered in the valley of the shadow. There is no attempt to belittle the evil of the present moment. But the psalmist carries his pain and heartache into the presence of God. He recalls what men have known of God in the past:

Our fathers trusted in thee;
They trusted, and thou didst deliver them.
They cried unto thee, and were delivered;
They trusted in thee, and were not confounded.

That was yesterday and this is today. God was able to help someone long ago, but here am I, today. Can God help me? The psalmist, feeling God-forsaken, turns to God and cries:

Be not thou far from me, O Lord:
O my strength, haste thee to help me.

Faith, which had seemed at such a distance, begins to surge back. The psalmist, whose lament begins in the valley of the shadow, finds himself singing from the mountain tops:

Ye that fear the Lord, praise him;
All ye the seed of Jacob, glorify him;
And fear him, all ye the seed of Israel.
For he hath not despised nor abhorred the
    affliction of the afflicted;
Neither hath he hid his face from him;
But when he cried unto him, he heard.
They shall praise the Lord that seek him;
Your heart shall live forever.
All the ends of the world shall remember and
    turn unto the Lord;
And all the kindreds of the nations shall
    worship before thee.

The reality of the moment — pain — continues unabated. Faith knows realities greater than anything the world can give or take away. But when faith fizzles out, what then? In the fourth word from the cross our Lord tells you that, when you think God has abandoned you, carry your despair to God.

There is no virtue in being discouraged. Everyone goes through that. The virtue comes in the way you handle your discouragement. Do you let it engulf you, or do you engulf it with faith?

Despair as a Part of Life

When we were little children, we knew the loneliness that comes from being misunderstood. During adolescence we felt that adult misunderstanding of us rose to a crescendo. Only when we ourselves become adult, and attempt to guide children through the perils of childhood and the temptations of youth, do we begin to realize that our parents and teachers understood us better than we thought at the time. Yet, for most of us the depths of despair come during mature life, and not in childhood.

Despair is the feeling that nobody understands or cares, not even God. When a person despairs, he wants to give up. He feels that there is no use in going on. This feeling is a part of almost every creative life. If an artist hopes to do more than travel in paths that others have worn smooth, he can be sure that many will mock and scorn. The scientist who first glimpses the vision of a new concept is often called insane. The social reformer finds his bitterest struggle not against the hostility of his enemies, but against the apathy of his friends. Everyone who dares to stand beyond the crowd learns that the crowd can be cruel to those who fail to conform. It is lonely, out where progress is made. Often the one who contributes most to humanity knows the deepest depth of despair.

We who follow the crucified Savior must expect tribulation. Our Lord promised as much. Millions of our fellow Christians are facing the problem of life in a society that denies God. Today a family in Hungary confronts this problem in its most acute form. When the Communists took charge of their country, the father was given a chance to declare himself in favor of the new government. He refused, and the next day he was deported to Siberia. His wife (perhaps his widow) and his children were thrown from their comfortable home. They live now in an attic. The oldest boy is ready to enter the university. The way is almost clear. He has passed the entrance examinations brilliantly. The government will pay his tuition, without prejudice because of the father. The boy has the ability to become a leading engineer. But there is one obstacle. Before he can enroll, he must sign a paper stating, "I am free from the foolish influence of religion."

What is the boy to do? How is the mother to advise? If he signs, as many of his friends have signed, he can prepare to enter an honorable profession. If he refuses to sign, he can sweep streets for the rest of his life. What would you tell your son? Deny your Lord and save yourself? Or deny yourself and take up your cross? It is easy for us to be bravely anti-communistic in a land where almost everybody is so. For those who must live with communism, Christianity comes at a high price.

Do you suppose the lonely mother in Hungary ever wakens in the night, crying, "My God! my God! Why hast thou forsaken me?" Of course she does. That is why the cross is relevant in human life today. Our Savior has plunged into the deepest blackness of human experience. He did it to lift us into the radiance of God.

What to do With Despair

It is no crime to despair. On the other hand, there is no virtue in feeling whipped and wanting to give up. The virtue all lies in what you do with the moments of despair that come into every human heart. Do you let them grow within you until they destroy you? Or do you carry them to God? Those who have contributed most to humanity have known discouragement and loneliness, but they have persevered when they wanted to quit. Anyone who tries to be a Christian today must know times of utter loneliness, when even God seems to have forgotten.

What does our Lord expect when He says, "Whosoever will come after me, let him deny himself, and take up his cross, and follow me" (Mark 8:34)? If a person takes up a cross, he will know pain. If a person tries to follow Jesus Christ, say in race relations, industrial relations, politics, or education, he may find himself out far ahead of the crowd, lonely, hooted at, mocked, and jeered. He will begin to wonder, "If God cares about what I'm doing, why doesn't He wake these people up?" He will catch a faint glimpse of Christ's loneliness.

In His fourth word from the cross, Jesus tells what you can do when the bottom drops out of life, when hope is gone and faith is gone. You can turn to the Bible and follow the guidance of Scripture through your problems as they have appeared in the lives of others. Our Lord was not the first, nor was He the last, to find help and strength in the 22d Psalm. Have you noticed how, in time of crisis, Jesus quoted from the Bible? When He was tempted in the wilderness, three alluring enticements were dangled before Him, and each time He found strength to resist by quoting God's Word. Again in His bitter agony on the cross, He recalled a passage of Scripture, and found strength for Himself, which He has been passing on to others ever since.

Note that Jesus did not say, "Let me go and look for a helpful Bible verse." He had taken seriously the example of the psalmist who sang, "Thy word have I hid in mine heart, that I might not sin against thee" (Psalm 119:11). He had lived with His Bible, and committed much of it to memory. When He needed the aid that God extends through the Scripture, divine help was at hand.

Jesus has set an example. In the days of His health and strength, He used His Bible. He read it, He thought about it, He talked about it. He learned its words and lived its message. Then came a time of despair, when the Son of God felt God-forsaken. But treasured in His memory was the thought He needed to carry Him through to spiritual triumph. Follow your Lord's example in the thoughtful use of the Bible, and you will find God's Word a lamp to your path even when no other light is shining.

The way to the Kingdom is steep and rocky, but it leads at last to the realm of eternal light. Sometimes the light ahead shines brightly, and we can see the way clearly. Sometimes we have only fitful glimpses of the light. Sometimes we cannot see at all, and we are lost. Jesus too felt lost. But in His heart He had hidden the compass that enabled Him to find the way again. The cry of dereliction is the fourth word from the cross, not the last. A few moments later, our Lord uttered a cry of need, then a shout of victory, before He commended His spirit into the hands of the heavenly Father. Before His mortal life was done, the Son of God realized again that the Father knows and cares when the light in our lives blacks out.

5

THE CALL FOR HELP

I thirst.

JOHN 19:28

As Jesus was dying on the cross, He developed an agonizing thirst. He had a physical need, which He Himself could not satisfy. So He called out, "I thirst." The Evangelist tells us, "Now there was set a vessel full of vinegar: and they filled a sponge with vinegar, and put it upon hyssop, and put it to his mouth" (John 19:29).

It would be cruel to offer what we call "vinegar" to a dying man. But the word which is translated "vinegar" can also be translated "sour wine," and I believe that is the meaning in this case. It is difficult to imagine why there should be a bowl of vinegar at the foot of the cross. But it is easy to picture a soldier, packing his lunch for the busy day on Calvary, and including a flagon of sour wine. When Jesus, in desperate need, cries out, "I thirst," the soldier compassionately offers Him a sponge soaked in sour wine, to cool His lips and to slake His thirst. I believe that this drink was offered in compassion, not in ribald jest.

A soldier was wounded in battle, and left behind as his comrades advanced. First came the blinding pain of the wound. Then shock set in. As the sun beat down upon him hour after hour, he knew all the fears that can enter the mind of man. Then flies came to torment him. As the bleeding of his wound continued, one feeling came more and more to dominate his mind — thirst. When the medical corpsmen

49

found him that evening, he had strength only to ask for water. He says that, looking back on his day of hell, his outstanding memory is the agony of his thirst. Jesus knew this agony, too.

Does God Have Needs?

We Christians believe that "God was in Christ, reconciling the world unto himself" (II Corinthians 5:19). To be sure, we have many and differing ways of expressing our belief. Sometimes in Christian thought the heavy emphasis has been upon the divinity of our Lord, sometimes upon His humanity. The religious conservative of today stresses the divine, the religious liberal stresses the human. Though each is right in what he stresses, each is dead wrong if he denies, or fails to emphasize, the opposite truth.

Sometimes Christian piety has so emphasized the Godhood of Christ that people have believed Jesus to be merely a phantom, going through the motions of human life, not a Man of flesh and blood, who could suffer and die. This mistaken belief, which the scholars call "docetism," gives men a Gospel high and lifted up, but out of touch with the problems of earth. Sometimes, in stressing the manhood of our Redeemer, people have denied His deity. This denial leaves us with "Christianity" as a magnificent ethical code, which is simply impossible, because it is out of vital touch with God.

The orthodox Christian believes that Christ is fully God and fully Man. When we think of Him in divine terms, we must always remember that God became a Man, a particular Man whose footsteps shook the floor, a Man who knew the pangs of loneliness, and the joy of human friendship, a Man who endured all the weakness and temptation that go with mortal flesh, a Man who could develop a hideous thirst while bleeding to death. Yet when we think of our Lord in human terms, we must always remember that even while the hands of Jesus were stretched out, nailed to the cross, the hands of the eternal Christ were spinning the stars in their courses.

The attempts to clarify the mystery of the Incarnation have not been successful. Some have sought the easy way out, denying either the divinity of our Lord or His humanity. The vast majority of Christians, faced with the facts of revelation and experience, have stubbornly clung to the full truth. The Incarnation is a mystery. We do not, indeed we cannot, comprehend it. Though the navigator does not understand the mystery of light, still he confidently steers his ship by the distant stars. The Christian has found the Incarnation of our Lord to be a mystery of light by which he can guide his life with perfect confidence.

Does God the Creator have needs which one of His creatures can supply. No, of course not. Could God the Creator become one of His own creatures, subject to all the natural and spiritual laws of human life? He could and He did. "The Word was made flesh, and dwelt among us" (John 1:14).

The mystery of the Incarnation means a great deal to me, and to every Christian who takes it seriously. It means that I have no sorrows God cannot understand, no pain He has not borne, no temptation He has not overcome, no joys I cannot share with Him. It means that I can take in a literal sense the song, "Yea, though I walk through the valley of the shadow of death, I will fear no evil; for thou art with me" (Psalm 23:4). My Lord knows the way through the valley. He has been there before.

As we look at the life of our Redeemer, we find Him with many human needs. He hungers and thirsts. He endures loneliness, grief, pain, and uncertainty. He is weary. He weeps. All of this is human weakness. It does not fit into our picture of God's almighty strength. The Apostle explains it this way: The eternal Christ, "being in the form of God, thought it not robbery to be equal with God; but made himself of no reputation, and took upon him the form of a servant, and was made in the likeness of men: and being found in fashion as a man, he humbled himself, and became obedient unto death, even the death of the cross" (Philippians 2:6-8). The expression "made himself of no reputation" can be translated more exactly "he emptied himself." Our Lord divested Himself of God's power and glory when He entered into human life. He left His throne and His kingly crown, and He accepted the crown of thorns, the pain, the shock, the humiliation, the buzzing flies, and the thirst of the cross.

Man's Dependence Upon God

During our Lord's days on earth He had needs, physical and spiritual. During our days upon earth, so do we. Our Savior's cry for help is a reminder that each of us has needs, physical and spiritual, that he cannot meet by himself. A Christian recognizes that he is completely dependent upon God, and partially dependent upon his fellow man. We teach our children to be independent, self-reliant, free — and rightly so. Our Creator, who made us vertebrate, expects us to stand upright. When the Lord gave us hands, He intended us to toil with them. We believe that the human parasite is far less than the person God requires man to be. In our attitude of strong independence is a lurking danger that we may forget our need for others, and for God.

Without God's creative and sustaining power, this world could not exist. Jesus tells us to ask, "Give us this day our daily bread" (Matthew 6:11). The prayer in no way excuses us from the obligation to toil and earn our daily bread, as long as we are able. The prayer is our recognition that God gives us the power to work, as well as the things with which we work. This ability, with every other talent, should be directed to God's service.

God has entrusted to us spiritual blessings, along with those that are physical. The Apostle says, "The fruit of the Spirit is love, joy, peace, long-suffering, gentleness, goodness, faith, meekness, temperance" (Galatians 5:22-23). We do not create love, joy, peace, and the rest. These are the by-products of God's activity in our lives.

The Heavenly Father, who has given us so many other blessings, offers us the supreme gift, our holy faith. Christianity is not a matter of man's fumbling after the divine. "God so loved the world that he gave his only begotten Son" (John 3:16). Christianity is God's gift to man. What sacrifice could we offer that would purchase the forgiveness of our sins? What strength have we to open the gates of heaven? Can any of us climb from human bondage into the glorious liberty of the children of God?

No, we cannot make the grade. Each of us has sinned and fallen short of God's glory. The Scripture solemnly warns that "the wages of sin is death" (Romans 6:23). This does not mean mere physical death. As the "life" that Christ gives is more than protoplasmic activity, so the "death" from which He saves us is more than stoppage of the heartbeat. Life means communion with God, now and always. Death means separation from God.

On the cross our Savior endured the pangs of physical and spiritual death, in order that we might enter into life. "The wages of sin is death, but the gift of God is eternal life through Jesus Christ our Lord" (Romans 6:23). We depend upon God for our salvation. We have not earned His love. He has given it to us. We have not paid the price of forgiveness for our sins. Christ has paid it in our stead. We have not pushed aside the gates of heaven. Our Lord has opened them for us. We must depend upon God for our physical being and for our spiritual life.

Man's Dependence Upon Man

The strong Son of God hung dying on the cross. His lips and His throat were parched. He called for help, "I thirst." Whom did He call? Did an angel descend to aid Him? It was a soldier of the Roman legion who answered our Savior's cry of need. Only when a person is unable to help himself can he, with self-respect, ask another's aid. Even the eternal Christ, who had laid aside His power and glory and hung helpless on the cross, did not think it below His dignity to call upon a man for help.

No man can finally rely upon himself. Each of us is a unit in the body of mankind. Each of us depends upon others. God brought us into the world through the agency of human parents, and a host of ancestors. Each of us grew in an environment, surrounded by all sorts of people who made a direct contribution to his life. We live in human society. The Christian contributes to society, and likewise he receives. Sometimes we Christians are most reluctant to admit how much we depend upon our fellow man.

One of the major problems a pastor faces is the difficulty of dealing with the friend who has fallen upon hard times. He needs financial help. Godly people have given the pastor money to use in meeting human needs, but the friend stubbornly refuses any assistance. He feels that there is some kind of taint about the receiving end of Christian charity. But charity is love for God so great that it overflows as love for man. Charity ennobles everyone it touches, both giver and receiver. When Jesus was in need, He called upon His neighbor for aid.

A problem that grows increasingly serious is that of care for the aged. Medical science has far outpaced our social attitudes. Many more people live to an age where self-help is impossible than was the case a few years ago. Pensions, social security, and the rest are well and good, as far as they go. Most churches have gone further, and provided homes for the aged, recognizing that people do reach a time of physical infirmity. As any minister will tell you, when he suggests that an aging friend apply for admission to such a home, the friend almost always answers, "What? Me? Accept charity?" Is it degrading to accept the love of God, even when that love comes channeled through human agents?

Ye Have Not Because Ye Ask Not

Man's deepest needs are spiritual, not physical. Important

as the body is, it dies; but the spirit lives on into eternity. As spiritual beings we need friendship, understanding, sympathy, love. All too often, we have not because we ask not. We build a wall of reserve about ourselves. Then we are surprised that no one penetrates the wall.

A doctor tells of a patient who came with a complaint of a cramping pain in the abdomen. After a thorough examination, the doctor said, "You are all tied up in knots. There is nothing organically wrong with you, yet. I believe that you have some deep worry, and I'm afraid that the pain will go on until you get the worry straightened out."

The patient thought for a while, then said, "Doctor, about ten years ago I got tangled up with a woman. It's all over. My wife knows about it, and she's been wonderful. But recently I became an officer in my church, and now this woman threatens to tell my pastor."

The doctor exploded, "Man, go tell him yourself. Sin is his business, the way sickness is mine. It's no surprise to him that people make mistakes and do wrong."

A few weeks later the doctor met his patient, a well man. For years he had been needing the kind understanding of a Christian friend, and he had been afraid to ask for it.

Our Savior founded the church upon earth, because people have spiritual needs that can best be met through human agents who are filled with the love of God. A pastor's supreme joy in life is helping his friends with the problems that confront them, bringing the light of our faith to bear upon human troubles, opening the channels of divine love. Sometimes Christians are reluctant to bring their problems to their church. They are ashamed to expose their failures. They are too proud to ask for help.

The quality of self-respect is good. But when we push this quality too far, it becomes something evil, which Christians call pride. Pride means confusing one's self with God. Pride is the temptation to go it alone, without calling on God or

neighbor for help. Only God Himself is completely independent. We are not God; we are creatures, totally dependent
upon Him, and partially dependent upon one another.

One need we have that Jesus did not have, and only one.
Our Lord was tempted in all points as we are, yet without
sin. The rest of us have sinned. If we are to know spiritual
life, we need to be forgiven. What must a person do to receive God's forgiveness? First he must ask for it. In the
privacy of prayer, when you are asking God to forgive, do not
be hazy and general. Be specific, giving names, dates, places,
facts, and figures. Bring into God's presence all the moral
wrong you would like to hide from yourself. When you see it
clearly, and confess it humbly, God will sweep it all away.
But first you must ask.

Christians are ready to forgive the repentant neighbor, but
sometimes they are remarkably unwilling to ask his forgiveness. Occasionally the neighbor is right. Only the one who
has been wronged can forgive. It is cruelly hard to swallow
pride, and go to the neighbor saying, "I was wrong. Forgive
me." No one likes to humble himself, but sometimes it is
necessary. Almighty God humbled Himself to bear the cross
so that you and He could be reconciled. Perhaps you need to
humble yourself and ask your neighbor's pardon, so that you
and he may be brothers.

The supreme offer of help through life's pressing needs
comes from the One who carried the burdens of this world's
sin up the hill to Calvary. Included in His crushing burden
was every bit of moral evil in your life. The Son of God
died on the cross so that you can be rid of the wrong that is
in you, so that you can become a Christlike person, a child of
the Heavenly Father. The fifth word from the cross is an
eternal reminder that, when a Christian genuinely needs the
help of God or his fellow man, he should ask for it.

6

THE SHOUT OF TRIUMPH

It is finished.

JOHN 19:30

The endless hours of suffering are over. The Savior is about to die. It was for this cause that He came into the world. Now He has completed the work His Father gave Him to do. He raises His voice in a triumphant shout, "It is finished."

During the past few weeks Jesus had been preparing His disciples to accept the need for the cross. They all shrank in terror from the thought that their Friend should suffer and die. Praying in the garden, Jesus confessed His own dread of the cup He must drink. On the cross He drained the cup to the uttermost dregs, and cried, "It is finished."

A steady undercurrent of Christ's teaching is that a person should count the cost before he undertakes a task. And when he has committed himself to the task, he should keep at it until he has finished. "No man, having put his hand to the plow, and looking back, is fit for the kingdom of God" (Luke 9:62). In this regard, as in all others, Jesus practices what He teaches. Our divine Redeemer came to the world to save sinners, and He remained in the world until He had done everything almighty God had planned to do to save those who are lost. When His days as a Man were ended, our Lord could cry out, "It is finished."

The Work of Redemption

Love's redeeming work is done. And what, precisely, is the

57

work that our Savior finished on the cross? When I ask this question of little children, they tell me, almost without exception, "He came into the world to teach us how to live." They are right, completely right, as far as their answer goes. Children know about teachers, and how important they are. They do not yet know the ghastly tragedy of sin, from which we need to be saved. When we think of Jesus as the Teacher, we are leaving unsaid the most important truth about Him, "that Christ Jesus came into the world to save sinners" (I Timothy 1:15). Jesus is not only the highest and best Teacher; He is our Savior.

How does Christ save? What is the connection between the death of one Man long ago, and the spiritual life of another person today? Devout people have believed that on the cross Jesus paid a ransom to Satan for the souls of God's people. Some say that He endured in our stead the wrath of God upon human sin. Others suggest that He offered to the Father satisfaction for the outraged moral law. Still others teach that He vicariously suffered for us the separation from God which sin always brings about. While certain of those beliefs are far more satisfactory than others, not one of them fully answers the question, "How does Christ save?" For the full meaning of the cross is to be found only in the heart of God. When we try to reach into God's heart, we are straining beyond our grasp. "O the depth of the riches both of the wisdom and knowledge of God! how unsearchable are his judgments, and his ways past finding out!" (Romans 11:33).

During this part of our eternal lives, we can never fully know what the Atonement means to God, nor can we completely envision the indescribable mystery in His plan of Salvation. To us, Christ's atoning work means at least this much, that God Incarnate became sin for mankind. Our spotless Redeemer subjected Himself freely, body and soul, to all that sin means. He drew it all into Himself, in soul and body, and offered Himself, thus stricken, to the Father.

> He was wounded for our transgressions,
> He was bruised for our iniquities:
> The chastisement of our peace was upon him;
> And with his stripes we are healed. (Isaiah 53:5)

Since we are healed with our Savior's stripes, we ought to
be living the lives of those who are healthy. Our Savior went
to the cross to transform us stingy, arrogant, self-centered mor-
tals into sons and daughters of God. The Redeemer has done
everything that divine love need do to help us become God's
children. Children, not puppets! Our Creator desires from
us, not the mechanical reaction of things to mechanical laws,
but the free response of healthy spirits to the Father's love.
Every atom in the universe responds instantly to the Creator's
will, but He has made us free to withhold our love from
Him or to return it. Our Savior died for us, so that we
should return God's love to Him, and returning live.

Jesus completed the task His Father gave Him. He laid
down His life for His friends, and He cried, "It is finished."

But Why the Cross?

Jesus said, signifying what death He should die, "I, if I be
lifted up from the earth, will draw all men unto me" (John
12:32). As a matter of present, visible fact, people of every
race and nation on earth today are turning to our Lord,
drawn by the spiritual magnetism that radiates from His
cross. But why the cross? Why must divine Love endure
humiliation and shame? Let us consider one significant
aspect.

Since God has willed to draw the world's people to Himself
in love, how better could He do it than with the cross? In
the fifth century before Christ, Aeschylus, the Greek
tragedian, wrote of Prometheus, bound and suffering. A
friend says to Prometheus, "Look for no end to this, your
agony, until some one of the gods appears to take your woes

upon himself, and of his own free will descends into the un-lighted depths of death." That is a hopeless moan in the darkness. Aeschylus knows that the gods of Greece can never be so concerned about mere people as to suffer and die in our stead. He has a wistful dream of what God might be. Yet he sees to the heart of man's need. He sees the one power strong enough to draw man from his bondage to evil and pain. He expresses a pathetic wish that God would apply this force.

The power that Aeschylus imagines is symbolic of the power that Isaiah and Hosea so clearly describe, the redemp-tive power of suffering love. This is the strongest moral force in the world. We know the destructive moral forces at work all about us, tearing down what others have built, poisoning what others have grown. Sometimes we forget that Christ came into the world to destroy the power of darkness, and that He destroys it with His cross. Evil men could nail Jesus' outstretched hands to the cross, and sneering watch while His life ebbed away. But those evil men could not overcome the love in our Redeemer's heart. His love continues through pain, embracing those who afflict the pain. This is the magnetism which attracts men of every tribe, race, nation, and tongue, the redemptive power of divine suffering love.

There can be no doubt concerning the power that radiates from the cross into the world. Here is the way one man describes the redemptive power of Christ in his own life. This man retired recently, after forty years as director of a down-town City Mission. In a letter to a friend he writes:

You ask why I spent my life in the depressing atmosphere of a City Mission. I was ordered there. Christ sent me. You see, He found me there, when I was a drink-sodden wreck. One night I went to the Mission for a bowl of chili. The evangelist's words penetrated my stupor. "Christ Jesus came to save sinners." The diagnosis fit me well enough; then I began wondering if the therapy would work. At any rate, I stumbled to my knees and asked God to forgive my sins and help me to live a decent life. I accepted Christ as my Savior. And that moment, addled as I was, I felt a physical weight lifted from my shoulders. It was the accumulated guilt of a decade. A few days later, as I was praying for Christ's guidance, He said, "I picked you out of the gutter and forgave your sins. Now get back to the gutter and raise your brother who is still wallowing there." You speak of the unpleasant aspect of Mission work. Have you ever thought of the joy that comes when Christ uses a human agent like me in salvaging one of my brothers? My work in the Mission was not dealing with human wreckage, but with potential sons of God.

The forgiveness of sins is the backward look of redemption. The forward look of faith means victory over temptation. You can try a moral experiment, whether you be a Christian or not. When you are tempted to do something wrong, bring before your mind's eye the picture of our Savior's cross. Do not try to explain the cross, do not argue about it, just look at it. The temptation will lose its power. It has been the experience of thousands upon thousands that the redemptive power of divine suffering love genuinely redeems.

Our Lord unleashes the force of divine suffering love from the cross. This is the magnetism that attracts people of every color and tongue to their Lord. In Christ's divine love, a love that continues through pain toward those who caused the pain, we have the redemptive force that has transformed lives, and will transform lives, until every knee shall bow and every tongue confess that Jesus Christ is Lord.

Take Up Your Cross

The cross of Christ is the highest expression of suffering love. Yet He who was crucified has commanded each of us in turn to take up his cross. Though we cannot scale the

heights of divine love, as Christians we must practice human
love. Sometimes it seems, though, that even within the
Church we use the world's weapons of bluster, threat, and
retaliation. The history of strife between denominations, and
within many denominations, is a sad commentary on our
willingness to follow the Lord of Love.

Looking at the Church today, one can see much cause for
gratitude to God. Along with what is good and strong, one
can see some grave weakness, where Christians have failed to
apply the Lord's teaching and method. Our greatest weakness is the lack of love for one another. We are willing to
distribute good advice. We are ready to criticize without end.
We are almost anxious to point to ourselves as glowing
examples of what the other person can become. But one
thing is needful. Sometimes we forget to love the other
person.

A distinguished liberal theologian, forgetful of his Lord's
example, refers to his more literal-minded brethren as
"wooden-headed." They, in turn, retort with comments that
would startle a pirate. A staunch defender of the faith says
to his brother Christian, "I will pray for you, but I cannot
pray with you." The Protestant unthinkingly takes for
granted all manner of evil about the Roman Catholic. Without a shred of evidence, one Christian accuses another of being a Communist. Was it for this that our Savior went to
the Cross? Did He not die to save us from such sins?

Jesus Christ lived and died in order that the power of
suffering love might do its work in the world. Love cannot
be bottled up, nor can it be stored within a human soul. It
is a living force. As you practice love, it grows. As you fail
to practice it, love withers. When Christian people have
practiced Christian love, they have found that God is able
to use human agents in His work of reconciliation. Fre-
quently, not always, God enters a human heart through a
doorway opened by Christian love. Often, not always, you

can see the transformation in a person's life as your love is stronger than his malice.

Two farm communities lie about five miles apart, under the same sun and clouds. The farmers in each district raise the same kind of crops. They face the same problems year in and year out. Half the people in one community are related to half the people in the other. The two neighborhoods are as much alike as neighborhoods can be, in all but the important respects. In one community is strife. The fire department, the school board, and the grange are always squabbling back and forth. In the other community there is harmony. People live like Christian human beings, co-operating, bearing one another's burdens, pulling the load together.

The difference between the two neighborhoods can be traced to the influence of one man, a minister who lived in the friendly community for many years. He was no pulpit genius, nor was he a church organizer. But one thing he did consistently and well. He reflected the love of Christ. He loved people. When he moved to the little church in the country, he found a congregation torn with dissension, in a neighborhood permeated with hatred. While he did not lack convictions, he loved both parties to every dispute and sought to guide them to a God-honoring decision. He loved people when they were lovable. He loved them when they were detestable, and sometimes they were amazingly so. He looked for the good in the meanest of them, and he encouraged the good in the best of them. He lived to see a community transformed. From the isolated church on the hilltop where he labored in love, a constant stream of young men and women has flowed into Christian vocations. Those who decided to stay on the farm are acting like Christians at home.

Perhaps to some it will seem a small achievement, to diffuse the love of Christ throughout a rural neighborhood. If enough communities were transformed, the transformation of the world would not be far behind. Jesus died, having seen but one sinner redeemed through the power of the cross, yet Jesus cried, "It is finished." Having loved His own that were in the world, He loved them unto the end. He carried His love through pain to death, knowing that the heavenly Father would use the cross to redeem and transform countless human lives.

Christ's earthly work is finished. Ours is not. As long as a human heart beats unwarmed with the love of Christ, our work is not finished. Jesus did everything that divine love need do to redeem the world. He left for us the task of reflecting divine love by the practice of human love.

7

THE PRAYER OF TRUST

Father,
into thy hands I commend my spirit.

LUKE 23:46

When the fever of life was over and His work was done, our Savior recalled the evening prayer of His boyhood days, and with this prayer on His lips, He breathed His last. Like our Lord's cry of dereliction, the evening prayer is a quotation from the Book of Psalms. The Savior quotes what today we call Psalm 31:5. In the liturgy of the Hebrews, a portion of the 31st Psalm is included in the evening prayer. My friend the Rabbi tells me that almost certainly this was part of the daily ritual during the lifetime of Jesus.

We can picture the family in Nazareth: Joseph, Mary, Jesus, James, Joses, Judas, Simon, and the sisters. Each evening, shortly after sunset, the family gathers, and the members reverently commend their spirits to God. Now on the cross we see the eldest Son in the family, carrying the heaviest load that ever man has borne, as the sun sets on His sufferings. Before Him lies the merciful release of death. Recalling the family prayer of His boyhood days, He says, "Father, into thy hands I commend my spirit." Jesus adds a word to the quotation, a word that embraces most of His distinctive contribution to the biblical concept of God. The last word from the cross, like the first, is addressed, "Father."

"Father, into thy hands I commend my spirit." Our Lord speaks to the almighty Creator of heaven and earth, the infinite, eternal God. Yet He speaks to God, and invites us to speak to God, in terms of family affection. When we follow Jesus in thus addressing our Maker, we are approaching the throne of grace with boldness, believing that on the throne is One who is even more than our Creator, King, and Judge. As Augustine wrote, early in the fifth century, "Thou hast made us for Thyself, and our hearts are restless until they repose in Thee." God created man to be His child. Sin destroyed this relationship. Our Savior went to His cross to restore it. As long as we struggle to remain outside our Maker's love, we shall continue to be restless, wistful, hopeless. When we commit ourselves to the eternal security of God, then we can face all perils and dangers of the night, calm and unafraid.

The Prayer Through the Ages

A few months after Jesus died, His follower Stephen was martyred for his Christian faith. The record tells us that as they stoned Stephen, he called upon God, and said, "Lord Jesus, receive my spirit" (Acts 7:59). Ever since that time, as men and women have faced the last earthly hurdle, Christ's followers have braved themselves with the same thought.

In 814 Charlemagne died, praying, "Into thy hands I commend my spirit." In 1170 Thomas A. Becket was martyred. Four armored knights came into the cathedral where he was at vespers. He descended into the transept to face his murderers. One Tracy struck him a blow on the head, and drew blood. As the archbishop was wiping the stain from his face, he said calmly, "Into thy hands I commend my spirit." In 1415 John Hus was burned at the stake. He was condemned as a heretic, crowned with a paper cap ornamented with "three devils of wonderfully ugly shape" on which was written "Heresiarcha." Men could kill the body of John Hus, but the old record tells us, as the flame choked him, with "a merry and cheerful countenance," he said, "Into thy hands I commend my spirit."

The list is almost endless of men and women who departed this life with our Savior's evening prayer on their lips. The list includes Martin Luther, Christopher Columbus, Cardinal John Fisher, who was put to death by Protestants for being a Roman Catholic, Bishop Nicholas Ridley, who was put to death by Roman Catholics for being a Protestant, Lady Jane Grey, Mary Queen of Scots, John Knox, and a host of others, who faced bodily death with a prayer taken from our Savior's cross.

Twice in my life I too have thought that I was about to die, and once the doctor thought so. Both times I uttered the dying prayer which Jesus entrusted to us. As far as I can recall, I was too tired to fret overmuch about friendships that would be interrupted for a while, too exhausted to be overly joyful about what lies on the other side of the divide. Having commended my spirit into the hands of God, I went to sleep and woke in this world rather than the next. When a person is dying, about all he can do is passively to accept the future with trust in God. On the basis of my experience to date, I can say that it is much easier to die trusting in God, than it is to live trusting in Him.

A Prayer for the Day

What does it mean for a living person to commend his spirit into the hands of the living God? In our Bibles we find our Maker no abstract deity away somewhere in an abstract Heaven. We find Him at work in the world, and we hear Him calling us constantly to live our faith. If our lives genuinely are in God's hands, then we must try to find and apply God's solutions to earthly problems.

Each morning when we waken in this world, we face grave problems. God gave us our faith as a means of solving our problems. From Christ's dying word we may learn the Christian attitude toward everything that people fear. The Christian antidote to fear is trust in God. Trust is an emotional attitude. No one pretends for a minute that trust is all

of Christian faith. Our faith is a total commitment to
Christ. It involves beliefs, which result in emotional attitudes,
and which lead to Christian action. So, as we think of
trust, we are not thinking about all of Christianity, but
about a most important part.

We face two especial dangers today which, we think, did
not trouble people in Jesus' time. One is a danger of our own
creation. The destructive power of our latest weapons is
simply incredible. The physicist says that a single cobalt
bomb, of sufficient size, could destroy all human life in the
United States. We have other weapons that are less dramatic
but equally lethal. We are beginning to think of the atom
bomb, the kind that was dropped on Hiroshima, as a humane
weapon.

The other danger is political. With a zeal that often
shames us, the Communists are spreading a new dogma
throughout the world. Their dogma despises God and
worships man. The Communist thinks of prayer as a weakness. Rather than looking to God, he teaches that man is
able to solve his own problems and to build paradise here
on earth. Although the working model of paradise currently
in operation does not appeal to some of us, the new dogma
is spreading.

Here we have two problems, quite possibly the most serious
that people on earth face today: destruction for the body, and
poison for the soul. The problems are new, up to date. The
solution we offer is old, and some will tell you it is worn out.
If our solution really is worn out, we may wonder why the
Communists save their most intense hatred for it. If trust in
God is powerless, why should anyone want to destroy it?

The Communist teaches that religion is the "opiate of the
people." It was a Christian clergyman who coined that
phrase, not to describe what Christianity is, but to warn of
the depth we may reach if we fail to commend our spirits
into the hands of the living God. For Christ has said,
"Come unto me, all ye that labor and are heavy laden, and

I will give you rest. Take my yoke upon you, and learn of me" (Matthew 11:28-29). Evidently the Savior does not think of "rest in the Lord" as an opportunity to relax and end our labors. A yoke is a means of doubling the load a person can carry. The Savior said of His church, "The gates of hell shall not prevail against it" (Matthew 16:18). Christ's church is militantly to batter down the defenses of hell. When we commend our spirits into the hands of God, we submit our lives to His care for time and eternity, but we also ask Him to take us and use us to accomplish His purpose on earth. Trust in God is both active and passive. Passively the Christian accepts the will of God. Actively he does the will of God.

We are to face the unknown future with confident trust in almighty God. Trusting Him for the outcome, we are to practice our faith. The problems we face today rise, not from political systems and nuclear reactions, but from human tyranny. That is, our fundamental problem is spiritual, and its solution must be spiritual. Faith is up to date. Though political systems have changed, and weapons have changed, people remain much the same from century to century. Man's basic needs, physical and spiritual, are the same today as they were in Jesus' time.

If the political terrorists of today are cruel, we cannot fear them more than the people of ancient Jerusalem feared the soldiers under Pontius Pilate. If our present weapons have an unbelievable destructive power, they cannot kill a person one bit more dead than could a Roman cross. Jesus lived in a time of political terrorism, when the future looked grim and bleak. He has a message for those today who must live with the same problem, of man's brutality to his fellow man. The last word from the cross is a reminder that our final security is not of this earth, but with God.

A Soviet Commissar of Education has stated the Christian's problem with crystalline precision:

We hate Christians. Even the best of them must be
regarded as our worst enemies. They preach love to
one's neighbor and pity, which is contrary to our princi-
ples. Christian love is a hindrance to the development
of the revolution. Down with love for one's neighbor.
What we want is hatred. We must know how to hate, for
only at this price can we conquer the universe.

What is the solution? Jesus expressed it: "Love your
enemies, bless them that curse you, do good to them that hate
you, and pray for them which despitefully use you, and perse-
cute you; that ye may be the children of your Father which
is in heaven" (Matthew 5:44-45). Our Lord does not promise
that love will turn each enemy into a friend overnight.
Rather he promises a spiritual and eternal outcome to the
practice of Christian love on earth. Beyond all this is the
earthly result.

God, who changed the blackness of the cross into light,
has changed the course of history again and again, through
those who have commended their spirits into His hands. The
Roman Empire slew Jesus, but in a few short centuries the
Christian Church grew and developed until it engulfed the
Empire. Just as it seemed that Jesus Christ was consolidating
His gains over Rome, a wave of barbarians from the north
came down and sacked "the eternal city." Many thought
that Christianity was doomed, but Christ proceeded to conquer the barbarians.

Our Savior is no weakling who needs to be protected from
every chill breeze. Christ is almighty. He came into this
world to conquer. Confident in the final victory of Christ,
the Christian carries out his humble, unspectacular duties of
each passing day in the spirit of Christlike love. He has commended his spirit into the hands of God. He seeks to apply
God's solution to the immediate, practical problems that
confront him. As his individual contribution to Christ's vic-

tory over Moscow, the Christian practices his faith completely, wherever he may happen to be.

The working solution to human evil is love. Christian love
is a reflection of that which is finally real and true, divine
love. The Bible tells us that, when all else about Him has
been said, "God is love" (1 John 4:8). This love is more
than a genial feeling toward the nice people in the world.
We see the love of God most clearly when Jesus prays for
those who are crucifying Him. When we commend our
spirits into the hands of God, surely we are committing ourselves to use God's solution to the problems created by
human evil.

The world's way is love for the immediate circle, indiffer-
ence toward the outsider, which quickly turns into hatred
when the outsider does wrong. Christ's way is love for the
immediate circle, love for the outsider, which remains love
when the outsider does wrong. This is the program Jesus
taught throughout His ministry, which He enacted upon the
cross, which He passes on to us. Some say that it will not
work, that you cannot overcome evil with good. They say
it is high-minded idealism, but impractical in a world like
this. Christ's program has conquered both the Roman
emperors and the barbarians from the north. It is working,
wherever Christians practice it today.

Love is God's solution to the world's problems. The
Christian has entrusted his spirit into the hands of love. In
doing so he has accepted the responsibility of practicing love
toward his friend, his neighbor, his enemy, and the stranger.
Often he thinks that it would be better to forget about love,
that a few short-cuts would enable him to reach the goal
much sooner. As he is faithful to his trust, he carries out
God's plans in God's way. And that is the way of love.

"Father, into thy hands I commend my spirit." This is a
God-given prayer for the evening. It is helpful too in the
morning.